TAKE FIVE

PROSE POEMS BY 5 POETS

poems by

Laura Baird
Deborah Brown
Barbara Siegel Carlson
Richard Jackson
Susan Thomas

Finishing Line Press
Georgetown, Kentucky

TAKE FIVE

PROSE POEMS BY 5 POETS

Copyright © 2020 by Laura Baird, Deborah Brown, Barbara Siegel Carlson, Richard Jackson and Susan Thomas

ISBN 978-1-64662-212-2 First Edition
All rights reserved under International and Pan-American Copyright Conventions. No part of this book may be reproduced in any manner whatsoever without written permission from the publisher, except in the case of brief quotations embodied in critical articles and reviews.

ACKNOWLEDGMENTS

We wish to thank the editors of the following publications in which these poems first appeared, sometimes in different versions.

Apokalipsa: "Statues Along The Street"
Cortland Review: "A Resonant Space"
Cutthroat: "A Little History" and "What The Spruces Might Say"
Truth To Power Anthology: "How to Live, What to Do," "Another Farewell to Truth"

Publisher: Leah Maines

Editor: Christen Kincaid

Cover Art: Five Orvietani by Frank Clemente

Author Photos:
    Laura Baird by Grace O'Connor, Grace Photography Studio
    Deborah Brown by Deborah Brown
    Barbara Siegel Carlson by Lily Stone
    Richard Jackson by Terri Harvey
    Susan Thomas by Peter Sills

Cover Design: Elizabeth Maines McCleavy

Printed in the USA on acid-free paper.
Order online: www.finishinglinepress.com
      also available on amazon.com

Author inquiries and mail orders:
Finishing Line Press
P. O. Box 1626
Georgetown, Kentucky 40324
U. S. A.

Table of Contents

PREFACE xi

I. The Nature We Are From

How To Live, What To Do (RJ) 1
On a Train Through Here (DB) 2
Valentine's Day (BSC) 3
The Night Sky (DB) 4
The White Spruce (DB) 5
After Threats of Nuclear War (BSC) 6
Surface of Things (LB) 7
Suburban Morning (RJ) 8
Isotopy Loops (LB) 9
Little Delta Wolves (LB) 10
Without a Map (BSC) 11
Dancing (ST) 12
Dreams Are The Sewer of The Soul (ST) 13
Syrian Elegy (RJ) 14
Nightly News (RJ) 15
Next to The Railroad Tracks (DB) 16
Who Loves Our President? (ST) 17
Hidden in The World (BSC) 18
The Gamble (LB) 19
Elementary Cosmology (RJ) 20

II. Spots of Time

Belief (RJ) 23
Caravaggio in The Cathedral of St. John (ST) 24
At The Edge (DB) 25
Bluster (ST) 26
Tucson Campground (DB) 27
Winter's Tale (ST) 28
Camping in Mount Laurel State Park, 2016 (LB) 29
What The Spruces Might Say (BSC) 30
On Newmarket Road (DB) 31

Two Galaxies (RJ) 32
Overgrowth (LB) 33
Statues Along The Street (BSC) 34
Nostalgia (ST) 35
Monroe, Georgia (LB) 36
The Perseids (RJ) 37
A Little History (BSC) 38
Norman Bates' House on Museum Roof (ST) 39
The Retreat (DB) 40

III. **The Unfathomable Life**
Journal Entry (LB) 43
Coach For The Abyss (ST) 44
Complimentarity (RJ) 45
Vacuum (ST) 46
Owl Tale (BSC) 47
A Resonant Space (BSC) 48
The Keys (RJ) 49
The Human Condition (LB) 50
A Recipe For Art (ST) 51
In The Five Towns (DB) 52
Amid The Crowd (BSC) 53
Another Farewell to Truth (RJ) 54

I came to explore the wreck.
The words are purposes.

—Adrienne Rich, "Diving Into The Wreck"

The poem must resist the intelligence
Almost successfully.

—Wallace Stevens, "Man Carrying Thing"

PREFACE

The fact that the title of this book is taken from the great jazz piece written by Paul Desmond for the Dave Brubeck Quartet's *Time Out* might suggest something about the structure. That album itself was influenced by a variety of sources from India, Turkey, Hungary, the Middle East, West Coast jazz, classical music, especially the Russian composers. In our own way we wanted that kind of mix to this form, the prose poem, which is itself in many ways undefinable. Besides a sense of jazz improvisation, we had in mind the traditions of epistolary exchanges as say with Dante and Cavalcanti or recently Bell and Stafford.

Gathered from a couple of years' work, we would agree on a rubric—place, travel, philosophical ideas that we would respond to from our own experiences but also keeping in mind the others to create a kind of loose dialogue. "Jazz is about freedom within discipline," Dave Brubeck once said, and that is what we kept in mind by maintaining a rubric but with our own styles and concerns.

Chronologically, we began with poems about travel, creating a conversation to exchange experiences often echoing a tone or image or perspective from one or more of the other's poems. After a few months of that we started to write about places closer to home such as Deborah Brown on her Warner, NH. For a while we added a formal element, the haibun. Following upon the prose a haiku provided an interesting counterpoint as is Susan Thomas' "Dancing" where the movement of the dance is counterpointed by the temporal movement of loss and then, with the haiku, a "runaway mind." We also thought that we might add personal responses to other writers and thinkers that relate their ideas to everyday concerns.

When it came to organizing the whole, we tried to keep in mind the eclectic mix of rhythms and musical themes in Brubeck's *Time Out*. We also vaguely wanted to echo the three part jazz concerto, So, the first section contains poems that tend to address who we are, the kinds of things we tend to notice (as for example, Laura Baird's "Surface of Things." Some of these poems are political as in Barbara Carlson's "After Threats of Nuclear War," while some others deal with social or ethical issues.

The second section deals more specifically with place based mostly on travel. Each of us had traveled here and abroad and had already written some poems based on our experiences. Some of these were written, as Wordsworth says, "recollected in tranquility," while others as we were at particular places.

The final section gathers poems that refer to thinkers and writers such as Heidegger, Pauli, Einstein, Pessoa and Rothko. One of the main issues here was to avoid writing a dissertation-like poem or a simple summary of a theory. The trick was to relate the idea to something everyday as the way "Complementarity" takes a theory in physics and applies it to the way we think. In many ways this was the most challenging section both to write and to organize.

In all we hope the whole book creates that sense of freedom within the [loose] discipline of the prose poem. What we hope for is a sense of structure, and within that a sense of improvisation, and a sense of an overall movement out of the self as it branches into the world. Paul Desmond once referred to John Milton's notion of what constitutes a good composition method—"wanton heed and giddy cunning." That paradox—and this is true of Milton's often serious and tragic writing as well as our own—seems fitting for the paradoxical vision of the prose poem, an attitude with which we addressed each other even in these sober times, and hopefully, the reader.

—Richard Jackson

I

THE NATURE WE ARE FROM

It is this backward motion toward the source,
Against the stream, that most we see ourselves in,
The tribute of the current to the source.
It is from this in nature we are from.

—Frost, "West Running Brook"

HOW TO LIVE, WHAT TO DO

There was the man playing his invisible violin on the street corner this morning, the roofers racing against the coming storm, the geese concerned with the right formation, the boy sling-shotting pigeons in the park, the man tasting his vintage cabernet, all in the midst of dreams that float like feathers from a bird the cats have caught, sayings that leak meanings they never intended, numbers too large to reveal what they hide like the Syrian homeless hiding beneath the shattered shells of their homes, and there is this box turtle eating the grapes I've left for him, circling the house like a planet or moon, though every moment contains all time for him as he follows star maps he's traced on the inside of his shell, whole constellations that lead him from one story to another, stories that say, yes, you can notice also this, the way the grass rises again after your step, how the rose petal leaves its sheen between your fingers, how the wind brings tickets for journeys hidden in words you have not yet discovered, stories that teach you it is all right to love the world again.

(RJ)

ON A TRAIN THROUGH HERE

Trees flash by winter's shortest days. On the hillside, a semi-circle of oaks in uneasy colloquy: what's next, what's next? A crowding of firs in thick undergrowth, some fallen, roots ripped up, bare limbs. More trees, more trees, these with branches held, guarded, high, over ferns. On a slope above the train, beds of flowers still interspersed. Next a bare field, then stumps, and a forest of trees prone, dead, broken down by what rough beast? And one trunk splayed out, branches denuded, yet stretched, heavy over the living. And those that swagger around an estate, sentries of space and luxury. On and on as the train shudders forward, through the heart of what we see

>and see anew when
>the conductor says "Mind the
>gap, mind all the gaps."

(DB)

VALENTINE'S DAY

The field across the street is filled with fog. The trees look haunted, water-stained. In front of me, red tail lights seep into evening's murky street. I don't see the pot hole. Far south of here where flowers have burst into full bloom and the ocean seethes, a boy daydreaming in class thought he heard balloons popping. Only it was a spray of bullets… Drops blur the windshield. Our tires slide down watery streets past a ghostly playground and branches

> bare and blushed in rain,
> while someone buried in us
> can no longer cry.

(BSC)

THE NIGHT SKY

That the new moon is never visible on the night of the New Moon. That when the sky is darkest you sometimes see fireballs flash. That through the night newly-bare branches reach towards the sky while my brother has electric shock therapy, convulsions he won't remember. Some of the extra connections in the brain are cut, the ones that focus on grief. While I pace, I look for Andromeda, so many light years away that the light I see tonight was emitted when woolly mammoths and sabre-toothed tigers roamed here. The next day my brother reaches out to me from the darkness he's wrapped in. He tests the light.

(DB)

THE WHITE SPRUCE

It grows only in Kyrgyzstan and only on the north side of peaks of the Achyk Tash Range. The needles would gleam in daylight, if sun shone in the shadow of these pinnacles, snow-covered despite signs of summer in the valley. In yards, no farmers near tin-roofed shabby barns, a predictable emptiness, except on the rutted road where a beat-up Soviet-era Lada sinks. I savor the solitude of this plain, where one spruce and my own steps seem the only living things. But of course that can't be right. Behind closed doors and covered windows are lives, faces and minds. The landscape shows only that things are not what we think, that we're not free of that forest locked in here by peaks, where a tree grows void of color.

(DB)

AFTER THREATS OF NUCLEAR WAR

It was almost time for something, but she didn't know what it was. There were signs: a card with a picture of Jesus left on a stone wall, a tree that looked like an upside-down belfry, how it seemed to be shivering from the inside, church bells in the distance whose echoes kept growing with the swaying of the tree. She remembered the vision she had of a tree shaking with birdsong, though there were no birds to be seen. She couldn't remember where. And then there was nothing but space.

(BSC)

SURFACE OF THINGS

Some days kicking at the surface, the water is a world of possibilities you can't see. My line is a needle piercing the bay. The shadow is a fish in dark water or a peacock feather under-wing shaft moving in small circles luring a speckled trout. There is a live oak with its branches cradled by metal arches intent on protection, so that when the winds come the tree will not be broken. Gourds now sun-streaked tan and spotted gray, have been vacant for years. While thousands of miles away a friend pushes a small strip of paper into the wailing wall. *I've written your name and a prayer.* The tomatoes we planted hugging the white wooden trellis. Their weight bends the lattice, until it breaks in the shape of a crucifix.

> Moss hangs from branches
> like ghosts enduring to see—
> belief enough, rising again.

(LB)

SUBURBAN MORNING

Now the light begins to harvest the darkness. Not even the orb weaver's web lets out a shimmer. You can hear the wings of the first hummingbird. For every whisper the vowels seem to fly off. How hard it is to imagine the stutter of the automatic rifle rippling over the cries of the concert crowd. Here the soul of the morning dove says something we'll never understand to the soul of the morning. There are fissures in the words we try to use. The watermarks of the past having their say despite what we want to write. The coyote in the woods down the ravine trying to speak over the ambulance on the next street. History's disobedient shadow on the garden wall.

(RJ)

ISOTOPY LOOPS

Things we can't explain happen slowly. The hugeness of what is real is just behind the far wall, like a booth with a two-way mirror, God's observation post. Or maybe the Big Bang. At the borders of our fireball, particles travel faster in paths of circles. Clouds of dark matter colliding hold the universe together, but there are no guarantees so it's nerve racking. Each night, our particular stone tilts on its axis, requiring a different arrangement of space. Moonlight feathers light into charmed gestures. In truth, we are double helix and the math of biochemical bits, counting the nuclear rhythms of pi-mesons, blaming conception on miracles. Mustard and tares grow wild, remnants of all that endures in the face of everything that changes. Time surrenders in a blur of incantations, unfolding like familiar voices. Somewhere a child is waking up, struggling to think clearly, and picturing a day creating a little something in coloring books. The child gives morning to her dolls and all the hours are births or gateways into magical thinking.

(LB)

LITTLE DELTA WOLVES

If it's a choice between the moon and the wolves, I choose the wolves. Last night, one wolf, half-blind came close enough to nuzzle my hand. His warm breath, warning against attempts to tame. The pack moving through dark woods harboring each one's ruin. Hearing the crows, seeing snow shining along beech branches in these dark woods, I'd like to know their abandon.

It rained all night. Wolves howling outside my window. Forest branches whip and sing with the wildness of ancient wolf spirits. I know wolves can't know the moon can never be a mirror for wolves or a self-portrait for any of us, always burning with her own intentions. Their howls can't release the moon from her rotation. Behind thunderbolts and ghosts, the disobedient moon is more stone than animal unwilling to accept the wolves shepherding warnings.

(LB)

WITHOUT A MAP

Among cigarette butts, bird droppings and crumpled tissues, I follow a bright leaf twirling down the street, curve past a sign blanked by the low sun, a storefront of mannequins, someone moving her lips to someone not there. I pass a dumpster whose contents overflow with boxes and building debris, a carwash with its puddles, a billboard with a young girl's mouth erased whose silence goes on unmapped. Like a leaf, a whisper past a locked firebox, people in heavy coats waiting for the bus, a church with no steeple in my home town, while thousands of miles away at a refugee camp in Bangladesh there's a muddy line to the latrine, and what gathers in the sky for a baby torn from her mother's arms. There is no country or religion for those screams.

(BSC)

DANCING

When joy left me I kept dancing anyway. I still heard muffled music and, drop by drop, I heard hope drip out of my happy life. When laughter came to my mouth I thought—why am I laughing? Sadness came with sickness and the imminent loss of friends. A child disappeared. A full grown man, but still, my child. The news was relentless and always bad. And if occasionally there was good news we didn't trust it. I kept on dancing, and I knew I was holding inside my body whatever was left to keep me going, waiting for something to return.

> You no longer love
> your runaway mind, so you
> dance it back inside.

(ST)

DREAMS ARE THE SEWER OF THE SOUL

after Fernando Pessoa

Who thought our dreams would turn out this way? My dreams are monstrosities pulling at the corners of my brain. In my last one, a slimy creature of the sea pulls me down to his domain until I wake as if asleep, but know nighttime is just a madhouse made of sleepless worms that eat what's left of our impossible dreams.

(ST)

SYRIAN ELEGY

A first light shoots through the holes in the wall. To simply name what's left of the family that the light tracks towards is to cheapen their memory. Their own names hover above them in the smoke. The shadows darting in and out of the buildings below have no idea. Someone fires over a broken wall without looking. Another has sat down, shaking, for he has lost control. He is not even embarrassed. It is a knowledge like the sound of the missile that appears later than the impact. He is focused on deflated soccer ball he mistook for crushed squash. The dust keeps kicking up as if it wanted to escape as a cloud. No one pays attention to the slogans that blow by like dried leaves.

> The words of distant
> negotiators hover
> as high as their drones.

(RJ)

NIGHTLY NEWS

Twilight spies on us from the tops of the pines. A few unidentified sounds break in from the growing darkness. Someone says we are not safe here. Someone says the moment has already been stolen. Vapor trails crisscross like broken branches. They have nothing to do with the news of the huge tube-shaped asteroid heading our way. Our own wishes limp for cover. On their way to us the stories die as they always do here. In a little while the yellow crime scene tape will wrap their words as evidence for what they did not say in time.

(RJ)

NEXT TO THE RAILROAD TRACKS

A pink sweater resembles a flower on a dark trellis, if you are staring down from the third floor through clotheslines. A lonely flower, singular, where pairs of pants, shirts are dark bits of green or gray.

The bulbs you planted in a yellow dish grow slender greens. Each tip thickens. White star-blossoms cluster under kitchen light and a scent—gardenias on summer night—floats, mid-winter, through an empty room.

(DB)

WHO LOVES OUR PRESIDENT?

The Chinese love our president. They love his yellow hair. They love his height and width, and especially they love his voice. They love how loud he talks and how he says whatever he wants whenever he wants to say it. They love Melania, too, because she loves their zoo. The Japanese, not so much. They think his hair is funny. They think his voice is funny. They think he is too fat and he speaks without thinking. They are reserving opinion on his wife. The Vietnamese are not saying what they think of our president, or maybe they have no opinion. The Filipinos and the North Koreans think whatever their dictators tell them to think. New Yorkers hate him. That's what he hears from his apartment. *New York hates you. Go away. We hate you.* All day, all night. That's why he plays so much golf.

(ST)

HIDDEN IN THE WORLD

The Buddha my mother bought years ago to decorate her garden now sits in my yard on a plank in a bed of wildflowers. One foot is missing, the other worn to a paw. The stone figure is pitted, with a smear of birdlime on its ear, lips chipped, eyes closed, mouth open in a state of perpetual laughter. The plank covers our septic tank buried beneath the flowers. One morning a feather pressed to the plank under an abandoned nest. Hard to tell if the birds in the branches above were crying or singing. My mother's forgotten the Buddha. Trucks barrel down the road. A plane drones over. Somewhere people are running in terror. Their homes on fire. Here the crickets are calling

>   to a lost feather.
>   Rain streaks down Buddha's belly
>   in a single tear.

(BSC)

THE GAMBLE

The last drop of truth empties into the lake. We spy on each other and the numbers on thermostats rise. Fossils talk of impact death with the resolve of rocks. Their skulls are sockets and mouths ripe with warnings: Nature's gamble. This world now is more stone than animal. Night is a static curtain of long-lost flickering memories. There's a war raging neighbor against neighbor. Our gamble. Back and forth, we exit our homes for work or perhaps shopping. The last good thing lowers its head making the sign of the cross. All of the past, held in an open hand. I could say to a stranger, I want to know a little more about you where time bends, stopping tail winds until suddenly, we are face-to-face. At this crossroads, the last days cross through what's been broken. Near the wall, mustard and tares grow wild, remnants of what endures. The heaven we chose is built out of wishes and ether. At dawn an elegy separates the things we need from the lingering ghosts we risk becoming. We pray in silence. High above the thistle bush, the moon hides and hums.

(LB)

ELEMENTARY COSMOLOGY

All of this happened when I knocked down the abandoned paper wasp nest, amazed at all the tunnels once crowded with workers heading towards a single center, a kind of geometry I once read for parallel worlds like the Koch Snowflake made by adding triangles at different angles so the center holds constant while the circumference, in infinite divisions, moves forever towards eternity, something our words try hopelessly to cast a net over, the mystery of this, the love of it, geese in formation, mustangs moving in a single wave, chimney swifts like a single flag waving through the night, everything around us suddenly echoing everything else, all of this while north of here hyenas were swarming with flags made of nightmares, swastikas instead of snowflakes, torches lit with hate, on this darkest night of the soul.

(RJ)

II

SPOTS OF TIME

There are in our existence spots of time,
That with distinct pre-eminence retain
A renovating virtue, whence—depressed
By false opinion and contentious thought,
Or aught of heavier or more deadly weight,
In trivial occupations, and the round
Of ordinary intercourse—our minds
Are nourished and invisibly repaired.

—Wordsworth, "The Prelude"

BELIEF

From here the world still looks upside down. The news records the blossoming silence after the bomb goes off. Words vaporize. There's a new honor killing someone tries to sell as love or religion. Below here, even the cemeteries try to shrug off despair. Maybe time is the lizard emerging from the cracks in the stone wall. If I didn't know better I'd say it was emerging from a dream that died here long ago. The courtyard pigeons grumble at anyone who doesn't believe. And anxious wind tugs at the St. Peter's sign. I think the old man against the wall must be him, must know what is coming as he tries to brush away the first stars with a wave of his wand.

—San Pietro in Montoio, Travestere, Rome

(RJ)

CARAVAGGIO IN THE CATHEDRAL OF ST. JOHN

In Malta, he paints the beheading of St. John the Baptist for the Knights Templar. He paints it brutal, real, no angels or marble columns. Just peasants committing a bestial act in an austere prison with indirect light and off-center subject. No one who sees it can look away from the simple peasant faces determined to perform a task they can't figure out. Their confusion is obvious, but something else has begun to darken their features. He understands this, sees it when he looks in the mirror. He thinks the Knights will protect him because of the painting. Maybe it is the best work he has ever done. But the painting betrays him. It shows the guilt tightening his own features as it creeps across the faces of the peasants. Soon it will happen again—another bar fight, another murder, another run for his life. And this time the Knights know exactly who he is.

—Valletta, Malta

(ST)

AT THE EDGE

Out there, at the edge of the solar system, the Kuiper belt—gritty dust, planetesimals and dwarf planets without homes—all named for a Dutchman who didn't believe the belt was there. I could live on the rim of that belt, far from the faces I saw at the shelter—the children who live on the outskirts, or on an icy moon of Jupiter, who don't eat lunch, don't eat supper. Where we live, there is no limit, just gravity that curves matter and space so they bend back upon us, a wire coat hanger twisted into a circle.

—First Congregational Church, Concord, NH.

(DB)

BLUSTER

We huddle at the bus stop against the tunnel of wind that explodes from the river and grabs at us around the towers. We're bundled in coats and scarves and hats, too wrapped up to meet each other's eyes. We're too swaddled to talk until the bus arrives and we start shedding pieces in the heat. We talk, we laugh, we sneer, and try to keep our tempers but we can't stop complaining of twisted characters, hideous speeches, terrible tweets, and even—treason. What will we do now? Because all of us are helpless and almost glad to bundle up, get off the bus and hit the wind.

—NYC

(ST)

TUCSON CAMPGROUND

It used to be an internment camp. Five thousand feet high, it's empty in March, except for a dented camper, a car and a tent, and trees that show fine green sprays. In the silence, blonde grass shudders on the hillsides. Along the dirt road, at each site, an iron grate for cooking, and the shadow of the Catalina Mountains, snow-pocked, impassable. I sit near a fallen wall and watch two squirrel eyes peer at me from the other side.

>   No sign of a prison, though
>   the campground is named
>   Gordon Hirabayashi.

(DB)

WINTER'S TALE

In the field between Wilmer's house and our house, the trees are fading without losing color. No killing frost to tell them, so no one knows winter is coming on—not the wild turkeys scratching for grain, not the little heifers in the still green grass, nor the bear foraging berries. Only Wilmer knows, tucked into his narrow bed, white hair spread on the pillow, white beard on top of the quilts.

—Vermont

(ST)

CAMPING IN MOUNT LAUREL STATE PARK, 2016

Winter winds cut through the shelter rafters—these same winds making measurable weather patterns over distances, across two states. Luminary lanterns, lining the trails leading around a lookout tower and downhill to the fire pit. Overhead, trajectories of stars are simply like us, entanglements of colliding entities along crossed paths. There's a map of space operating inside my head, for figuring out what to do from here. I believe stories I uncover from the past show me how to see through your eyes. Faint as the sounds of breath hitting the surface of love against this constant variable of time, dreams and memory of travels, knitting us together into this dream field. Dawn rushes in early, dividing the world.

(LB)

WHAT THE SPRUCES MIGHT SAY

We're not ever leaving, although the tundra is spongy in the summer light and our roots are shallow, but in the long darkness the squirrels crawl out of their holes only to shiver and scurry back under us, while we leaning in every direction watch the sky's apparitions. You may wonder why. Maybe we're messengers, our bodies spindly and stunted under those vast beings divining us, pouring us into eternity.

—Arctic Circle, Alaska

(BSC)

ON NEWMARKET ROAD

The car's rear tire catches a chipmunk. Tossed up, it spins for an instant before it drops. Along the winding road into town, a raccoon carcass, larger and bloodied; a squirrel, a woodchuck. It looks like we're waging war, although we usually slam on the brakes and swerve, risking collision. The cats we've lost refused to come in at night. A gleeful dog stuck his neck into a trap set for a fox. All winter, mice scuttle into the kitchen. I rolled over three cars myself, walked away, no more or less unhinged than before.

—Warner, NH.

(DB)

TWO GALAXIES

The woman watches the fire juggler in the piazza below spin twin galaxies from her outstretched arms. The tourists in the piazza don't know she is there. She's not sure herself, living in the distant memory of a memory. Every time she wakes and comes to the window something has disappeared into the broken wormholes of her mind. She half shutters the window. Every word is an invention she's not sure will work. The galaxies merge, then split apart. She remembers in that flash the secret word she protected with the other girls, like an ember still trying to glow. The lighted mosaics of the Chiesa Santa Maria hover over everything as if they were beyond this tiny universe. She no longer is sure what it means, but what it means is all the world she has.

—Piazza Santa Maria, Travestere

(RJ)

OVERGROWTH

In the woods we return to reason and faith.
—Ralph Waldo Emerson

Abandoned washing machines, wild plum trees and crumbling chimneys in the midst of these grasslands that now furnish cover for quail. I wander into the stream's bend and cast my patterns upon river streams, and my patterns refuse drift, or maybe find slower waters, back pools with rainbow tips. I let the outside world in slowly. There are open questions, me resisting. I could move fences, until nothing is left to tether. Freed by the river's forward moving, until all things are unsettled in me.

(LB)

STATUES ALONG THE STREET

At night, the cobblestones gleam with the secrets of statues. Many are faceless. Some look wounded. Others have missing limbs. I drop a coin into the cup of a man sitting on a blanket along one of the narrow streets. He has a blue bag tied around his stump. He nods softly. People break people like they're stone. Maybe he hears the light clink that drops between the cracks. There is a secret buried in the face of the broken man watching the street all day.

—Ljubljana

(BSC)

NOSTALGIA

Years ago we used to stay in a rundown hotel on the rue St. Benoit. Every night we came home from cafés at St. Germain des Prés—or from the Metro, after nights at African tango palaces or Gypsy clubs near République. We were always tired, a little drunk, so we took a shortcut through a street we called the Rue de Merde, where old ladies in their nightgowns walked their dogs late at night. We tried to avoid them in the dark, like people leaving the Belle Équipe or the Bataclan last week. Only they weren't laughing or sauntering down the rue Jean-Pierre Timbaud. They were screaming, crying, running, falling—those who could escape. They were avoiding bullets and corpses. Watching them on the news last week, we longed for the quiet nights of old ladies and their poodles, committing silent acts of public indiscretion on the innocent streets of Paris.

—Paris

(ST)

MONROE, GEORGIA

Landscape pathways are the distance no one wants to see. What people don't want to hear happens in the small things. What people want to hear is always silent, like charred embers forming the slightest sign of enduring left after flames of a bonfire. There in the flames, leaves vanish, and I see in their absence the super moon. This moon has instincts, it faces and stares, as you stare across the way, fingers in your pockets, making an escape to the bedroom. On the walk back to the house, I'm giving thanks. Prayer, open to anyone willing to enter there. Moving me back to a better place than I remember. The darkness collecting the fields.

(LB)

THE PERSEIDS

A few fireflies seem fooled by the meteors that slash through the dark like unfinished ideas. A few lights spark on the corrugated surface of the water like silver fingerlings. This is the way mirrors, too, empty themselves of their secrets. We say that the trees point to where the wind is going as if they chose to do so. This constellation was originally a Babylonian old man who lost his way. Now and then the lights from a plane carry off their own dreams. The latest theory is that the empty spot in space is the doorway to another galaxy. So it is we are carried off by one idea or another as if they were places to visit.

—Desoto State Park, AL

(RJ)

A LITTLE HISTORY

Someday my body will be the same color as a November leaf or the sparrow that just hopped down from the iron anchor set on a platform in the city square. The anchor is painted black, faintly shining in the clouded afternoon. A child tries to climb up on it and slides down again, falling into the rust-colored leaves. The anchor is fastened to a chain bolted to the platform. Where is the boat it once held? The sea it once touched? Now the child is playing in the leaves, the sparrow flying away, the anchor forgotten…

—*Ljubljana*

(BSC)

NORMAN BATES' HOUSE ON MUSEUM ROOF

We know the setup—Janet Leigh in the motel shower, Tony Perkins upstairs in the mansion, with the skeletal remains of his mother dressed and seated in a rocking chair. But, in Psycho, it's the basement that brings on the real horror. It's always about the basement, always what's underneath us. But here, on the roof of the Metropolitan Museum of Art, there's no basement below us. Downstairs is the museum's second floor with Van Gogh, Manet, clinging to the walls. Velázquez and Goya are just down the hallway, protecting us from evil and guiding us toward the Grand Staircase. But here, on the roof, there is only the façade of a red Gothic house. Something about it repels us but also draws us in. We fear it because we know it—an image Hitchcock has planted inside us. And, of course, we aren't alone on this roof. We share our fear with everyone else. We creep up to the house and laugh at ourselves as we look through the empty windows and into our mindless terror.

—NYC

(ST)

THE RETREAT

Bricks old as orphanages. "Put your scarf in the locker. Your purse, too. No phones." Through a locked door up a staircase to another locked door to an LGBTQ ward where someone wants to be referred to as "they" and another wanders in a bathrobe because his dresses and makeup haven't arrived. There are walls and more walls. The inmates lounge, plump with hunger. My brother listens to the stories painful and sad as his own. A man asks me for help fastening his grandmother's pearls around his neck. Walls and more walls. It's darkening and there may be no windows. My brother doesn't want to go outside, he says, though it is a mild November day. He feels safe here, safer than in my house. I've brought nothing—not a gift, not the mail that arrived for him. I've brought nothing, the nothing that could not matter.

—Brattleboro, Vermont

(DB)

III

THE UNFATHOMABLE LIFE

For all its charms, the island is uninhabited,
and the faint footprints scattered on its beaches
turn without exception to the sea.

As if all you can do here is leave
and plunge, never to return, into the depths.

Into unfathomable life.

—Wislawa Szymborska, "Utopia"

JOURNAL ENTRY

There are two ways to be fooled. One is believing what is not true. The other is not believing what is true.
—Soren Kierkegaard

We are heading towards the apocalypse, two hurricanes, two earthquakes and a volcano erupting, or, maybe the world isn't ending, only the world as we know it. No flooding here, as I navigate muddy fields wearing muck boots. I try to stay a half-step ahead, improvising the possible plot lines. I surrender to hay bales and pastoral grandeur in praise of the discipline of farm work. This is how your life turns out. The clashing of habits meeting in the shadows. Today's news stories are a consequence of this very same separateness and the past remains its own ongoing war. My thoughts drifting, like black smoke crossing the moon and down through pine trees.

(LB)

COACH FOR THE ABYSS

> *I see life as a roadside inn where I have*
> *to stay until the coach for the abyss pulls up.*
> —Fernando Pessoa

The coach stops every day, almost always with terrible news. Jeffrey is dead. And Francoise has dementia. Some rogue superpower might declare war on us or maybe we'll attack them. Sometimes there's news we want to hear: Kahlil isn't getting deported after all. Willie passed his swim test.

I never get on that coach, no matter how tempting it looks, all plush seats and clean windows. You can't imagine where it's going to take you. I go for the scary subway or the filthy bus. I always climb out the window or sneak out the back door of the inn. You don't want them to see you coming or going.

(ST)

COMPLIMENTARITY

How, in physics, two opposite things can be true at once

Thinking he is alone in the park he thinks of the mind as a seesaw where the two children rock back and forth. On the one side he is still alone in the park, on the other side he rises above even himself. In that version he sits alone with the buzzard in a dying maple. This is not the world he wanted to escape into. The day wears itself out like a used toy. The wind twists through the trees. One thought follows another with relentless regularity. He wants to erase himself into another future. This is when he calls upon us, because it is we who have been thinking this. The mind is a clone of itself.

(RJ)

VACUUM

> *Why are there beings at all*
> *instead of nothing?*
> —Martin Heidegger

Why dogs or cats? Why jaguars, rats, parakeets, humans? Why not random chromosomes flying apart? I want to be vapor, rising like river smoke in the early morning. We are all these molecules bunched up together, clinging for dear life. Why so dear? We might suspend ourselves anywhere, careless of feeling, careless of thought. We could care less about everything if we just learned to repel—going our own way to nowhere, for no reason in no time. How lovely to be nothing, with no country, continent, cosmos, to which we pledge allegiance. To be a black hole—still and invisible, timeless in space.

(ST)

OWL TALE

> *...into the Mind of Man—My haunt*
> —William Wordsworth

The owl had been living in a cage at the school, and it was my turn to bring it home for the night, so the principal put it in a large wooden crate that looked like a coffin without a lid, and it took two people to carry it to my car, though the owl didn't seem to mind, its soft hooting almost a purr. I dragged the box into the yard where it would have to stay for the night. I thought tomorrow to move it into the bathtub. Just as I placed it under the flowering dogwood, the owl tried to grab me, its toes grip my arm as it spread its wings in silence and looked at me with piercing, ancient eyes as if to say, where are you flying off? But the eyes had no eyeballs—they were like tunnels to a scintillating brightness I had to travel through to understand its hunger.

(BSC)

A RESONANT SPACE

> *Let's suppose there had to be one who opened her eyes and looked all around and saw who she loved without end.*
> —Dara Wier

for Gela Pisarova

Her rural scenes in their luminous shades take up every space on her walls. The canvases are made of linen that grew in a field of flax, its warm earthy smell steeped in summer's white nights. The paintings depict women and girls hauling grasses, or washing linen in the lake, or hanging the sheets on a line to dry in the field. Faceless, these brightly dressed figures seem to drift, translucent through the frame. But something hides in them as the memory of light in a dying leaf. Maybe the ghostly city the artist escaped when she went to live with her grandmother during the Siege. Or the peat she dug till her fingers bled as she imagined her parents still alive by the freezing window, every part of her trembling and mute as she waited to hug them again. Something wants to brush us away—or hold us where the flax flowers still rise and breathe on deep moonless nights.

(BSC)

THE KEYS

> *I want to possess the atoms of time*
> —Clarice Lispector, *Agua Viva*

As the earth turns away from the sun, a few cumulous clouds glow gold at the edges promising what they can't deliver. Another darkness sifts down upon us. The last chimney swifts take their secrets back to their own darkness. There are still a few signs to decipher. The crickets adjust our watches by the weather. The spider maps our universe further than we can see. The moth at the lamp reads our future in the directions the flame jabs. On the new mown field two rabbits face off, then jump over each in some coded way until they scamper away into the underbrush. Do you think I meant these as metaphors for what we don't know? No, I am sitting here with grief, with this set of keys left by a dead man that were never intended to open any doors.

(RJ)

THE HUMAN CONDITION

> *A human being is part of the whole, called by us "Universe." He experiences himself, his thoughts and feelings as something separated from the rest—a kind of optical delusion...*
> —Albert Einstein

I don't mind being compared to animals, mythical creatures, historical figures, movie icons, characters from novels, and elements from the periodic table. Only one thing agrees to repeat. Living: our single right. A butterfly wing, a tatter in blue and black becoming dust, disappears through my fingers. A cotton mouth I mistook for a sheath of tree bark swallows a bird. Paint your favorite scene, minus the people. Make an educated guess about cloud-lines and other infinite worlds. Position the landscape in front of the picture window. Step back and imagine yourself there, long after you've lost track. It is almost dusk. My dream-life filling with whatever I put in until what is seen is only what I've known. Figures appear and disappear, surfacing like vacant faces of past lovers, at the foot of the bed.

(LB)

A RECIPE FOR ART

> *I'm interested only in expressing basic human emotions—tragedy, ecstasy, doom, and so on—*
> —Mark Rothko

His dark palette starts in preoccupation with death. He adds irony and chance, the tension of curbed desire. Now we see how blue is held in a world of plum. Brown suspends it in the air, elevates its mood, almost makes it tingle. Brown is resolute. We depend on it to hold giddiness in check, as we heave relief in the heart-thumping leap from a sea of plum that almost swallowed us whole. What kept us in that eternity was hope, Rothko's last ingredient. Hope, he said, "to make everything endurable."

—Pace Gallery, NYC

(ST)

IN THE FIVE TOWNS

All the animals, the plants, the minerals, even other kinds of men, are being broken and reassembled every day...
—Thomas Pynchon

In the Vernazza town square now, the dry-stone is so dark the hooves of the donkeys that carried it here echo. All the stone in the never-finished Santa Spirito church is a cross someone has walked on. None of the towns is a place where you can hide from the past. A dislodged mountain once covered Vernazza. Bunkers next to Monterosso's white beach were bombed by the Allies. Corniglia sat safe on its harborless hill. It's like the myth in which one sister drowns, another thrives, a third disappears into the hills. Today I am safe in these hills where a repaired, but still armless, statue of Neptune holds a dance floor on its back.

(DB)

AMID THE CROWD

There is in you what is beyond you.
—Paul Valery

Just past displays of fancy desserts and ornate masks in shop windows, an African man stands along the pavement selling leather bags on a blanket. He looks between you and the next passerby. Below, a gondolier pushes an old couple along in a boat. A bottle floats by in the wake. Who tossed it into those stricken waters? We walk through the ghetto and leave through the open gate, cross a few bridges, open the heavy door of the dimly lit Frari Basilica and come to the painting of the Assumption of Mary, its brilliant backlight and God's darkened face appearing to lift her, while on the other side of the wall a cellist plays out of the body's longing for oneness.

—Venice

(BSC)

ANOTHER FAREWELL TO TRUTH

> *Politics can no longer be thought of in terms of truth.*
> —Gianni Vattimo

The late sun bleeds its own light across the surface of the water. A yellow butterfly sips a little life from the edge. Someone has left an out-of-date history book on the bank. Beyond these hills the winds are trying to decide who controls the dust they kick up out of the ruins they have made. The tiny lizard with its tail chewed off has a question we'll never hear. A cloud of gnats keeps shifting direction over the surface. Each evening I understand less of why we are here. It is as if our shadows slipped downstream without us.

(RJ)

THE POETS

Laura (Behr) Baird was a *Third Coast* finalist and has published in *The Cortland Review, Numero Cinq, Canyon Voices, vox poetica*, among others. Her work also appears in two anthologies, *Paddleshots: Selected and Bottled by Pretty River Arts,* 2016, and *The Heart's Many Doors: American Poets Respond to Metka Krasovec's Images Responding to Emily Dickinson.* Laura lives in Montgomery, Alabama, with her husband, two daughters and step-daughter. As a psychotherapist, she has been in private practice for 25 years.

Deborah Brown's new book, *The Human Half* was published from BOA Editions in 2019. Her first book *Walking the Dog's Shadow,* was a winner of the A. J. Poulin Jr. Award from BOA Editions and of a New Hampshire Literary Award for Outstanding Book of Poetry. The title poem of the collection was awarded a Pushcart Prize. She edited, with Maxine Kumin and Annie Finch, *Lofty Dogmas: Poets on Poetics* (Univ. of Arkansas Press). With Richard Jackson and Susan Thomas, she translated the poems in *Last Voyage: Selected Poems of Giovanni Pascoli* (Red Hen Press). She lives in Warner, NH.

Barbara Siegel Carlson is the author of poetry books *Once in Every Language* (Kelsay Books 2017) and *Fire Road* (Dream Horse Press 2013), co-translator of *Open: Selected Poems and Thoughts of of Srečko Kosovel* (2018) and *Look Back, Look Ahead, Selected Poems of Srečko Kosovel* (Ugly Duckling Presse, 2010) and co-editor of *A Bridge of Voices: Contemporary Slovene Poetry and Perspectives (Kindle, 2017)*. Her poetry and translations have been published in *Cortland Review, Mid-American Review, Salamander*, and elsewhere. Carlson serves as Poetry in Translation Editor for *Solstice* and teaches in Boston.

Richard Jackson has published twenty-five books including fifteen books of poems, most recently *Broken Horizons* (Press 53, 2018). His own poems have been translated into seventeen languages including *Worlds Apart: Selected Poems in Slovene*. He was awarded the Order of Freedom Medal for literary and humanitarian work in the Balkans by the President of Slovenia for his work with the Slovene-based Peace and Sarajevo Committees of PEN International. He has received Guggenheim, NEA, NEH, and two Witter-Bynner fellowships, five Pushcart Prizes and has appeared in *Best American Poems '97* as well as many other anthologies. In 2009 he won the AWP George Garret Award for teaching and writing.

Susan Thomas' first poetry collection, *State of Blessed Gluttony*, (Red Hen Press, 2004), won the Benjamin Saltman prize. She has also won first prizes for poetry from the *Iowa Poetry Review*, *USC* (Ann Stanford Prize), *Spoon River Review* and *Mississippi Review*. Her poetry collections, *The Empty Notebook Interrogates Itself* (2011) and *In the Sadness Museum* (2017) were published by Fomite Press. She has also published two chapbooks, a collection of short stories, *Among Angelic Orders* (Fomite Press, 2014), and is co-translator with Richard Jackson and Deborah Brown, of *Last Voyage,* a collection of Giovanni Pascoli's selected poems, (Red Hen Press, 2010).

www.ingramcontent.com/pod-product-compliance
Lightning Source LLC
Chambersburg PA
CBHW020254090426
42735CB00010B/1922